Fight
<u>NOT</u>
Flight!

The Key To Stopping Anxiety

Boyd Brent

Contact: <u>boyd.brent1@gmail.com</u>

This book also includes:

Fight

<u>NOT</u>

Flight!

The Key to Preventing Panic Attacks

55-86

Introduction

Most people are aware of the fight or flight response. It's the term we use when we refer to our primitive survival instinct. When we feel threatened, our fight or flight response kicks in, and makes us either want to fight the perceived threat, or else take flight from it. When it comes to anxiety, you can forget about fight. Whenever you feel anxious, it's because <u>flight response</u> chemicals are being released into your mind/body system.

<u>Let's flip the coin from Flight to Fight</u>
The word 'fight' brings with it a world of negative overtones. However, when it's used in the context of overcoming anxiety, it refers to flipping the coin from flight over to fight, and utilising the resulting feel-good endorphins to defeat anxiety. The ability to do so is a life changer, providing the confidence to enter any situation (or face up to painful memories) knowing you have the skills at your disposal to stop any resulting anxiety in its tracks. This short book provides the easy to learn, <u>physical skills</u>

you need to achieve this from today onwards. I developed the skills you're about to learn as a means of overcoming my own battles with anxiety, and then went on to teach them to clients who visited my clinic in London from afar afield as the USA and Australia.

One

An Overview of Anxiety Free-Fall

Anxiety Free-Fall

You're feeling okay when, as if from nowhere, you experience a pang of anxiety, a sudden butterfly in your stomach. A voice in the back of your mind basically asks: "Are the things associated with this pang of anxiety a threat to you?"

Your anxiety intensifies, so you take deeper breaths to compensate, sucking more butterflies into your stomach, and your face adopts an anxious expression.

The voice in the back of your mind probes you again, asking: "Is there ANY CHANCE that this anxiety (and the things associated with it) are NOT a threat?"

Your growing mental and physical distress sends the clear reply: "No! There's no chance whatsoever!"

Your flight response is now fully activated, flooding your body the chemicals that are entirely responsible for making you feel anxious.

This process of Free-Fall is a vicious circle. Without a different on-the-spot response to the question that triggers it – one that sends a message of reassurance: "I'm fine! I have no need of my flight response!" – this process of free-fall will continue to occur.

Two

A New Way Of Responding To Anxiety

Millions of years of evolution has taught your mind/body system to trust your <u>physical response</u> to the things you encounter (this includes your thoughts and memories as well as things in the outside world) as to whether it will either:

A. Activate your flight response, releasing anxiety causing chemicals into your system that make you want to take flight.

Or B. Treat you to exhilarating, feel-good endorphins that make you want to seek out the experience again.

The good news is that your mind/body system has evolved to trust your physical response to your thoughts, memories and daily encounters completely. Why is this good news? Because it has no idea that you are about to learn the skills necessary to send it the positive physical message that tells it that you <u>no longer require your flight response</u> regarding

8

the issue/s that are currently making you anxious.

It's time for your long overdue introduction to the muscles that, for the first time, are going to enable you to send this message <u>wherever and whenever</u> you need to: the aptly-named Message Muscles.

Three

The Message Muscles

The Message Muscles are all important when it comes to defeating anxiety. They are the muscles that your mind/body system monitors to gauge how you feel about what you're facing or thinking about. The movement of these muscles informs it whether you're enjoying something, this includes your thoughts and memories, or feeling threatened by them. For the former you receive an injection of feel-good endorphins into your mind/body system, and for the latter you're treated to those flight response chemicals that are responsible for making you feel anxious. You're about to learn how to send the former, positive message that neutralises fight or flight and provides feel-good endorphins.

Our Message Muscles are located in three areas in our bodies:

Message Muscle no. 1: the Face
The most obvious, but by **no means the most important,**

are the muscles in your face, which conspire to contort your features into an expression of anxiety. This communicates one thing to your mind/body system: "Yes! I feel threatened and need my fight/flight response!" The facial muscles are very small-fry, however, when compared to the second message muscle, and it's no accident that it's one of the biggest and most flexible muscles in the human body: the diaphragm.

Message Muscle no. 2: the Diaphragm

Your diaphragm is located inside your rib cage, resembling a giant elastic band that stretches horizontally from one side of your rib cage to the other. Whenever you breathe in, your diaphragm moves down and assists in sucking air into your lungs as it does so. The longer you inhale, the further your diaphragm travels down towards your waist, and the tenser and more uncomfortable you feel.

Take a long, slow, deep breath.

Unpleasant, wasn't it? This is because when we breathe in, our diaphragm is pulled down and stretched into its most taut position. When we breathe out again, we experience a feeling of relief. Much of this relief is due to the diaphragm moving back up into a relaxed position. A sudden and pronounced upward movement of the diaphragm is key to switching off the fight or flight response in favour of feel-good endorphins. More on that shortly.

Message Muscle no. 3: the Abdominal Muscles

The third and final set of message muscles are the abdominal muscles. The abdominal muscles are as important as the diaphragm in sending a message that convinces your mind/body system to manufacture feel-good endorphins. In these fitness-obsessed times, we are all aware of where our abs are located, but let's reacquaint ourselves with them now. Bring a thumb and forefinger on the same hand together so that they touch, then draw them apart slowly to create a prong. Take this prong (your thumb and forefinger) and place it against your abs (horizontally) either side of your belly button. Now exhale forcibly and feel how your abs move inwards as you do.

An important realisation

Whenever we are involved in an enjoyable, uplifting activity, the emphasis of our breathing is ALWAYS on the exhalation – when we laugh, cheer, sing, whistle a tune, or groan because we're enjoying a good massage. During all these activities (and ANY OTHER pleasurable activity you can think of), the emphasis of our breathing is *always* on the exhalation, never on the inhalation. Let's take this analogy to its ultimate conclusion: the Roller-coaster Ride.

Four

The Roller-coaster Ride

Some people love roller-coasters, getting a high when riding them, while for others they can represent a nightmare. What dictates why some people love the feeling of that first uncontrollable plunge, while others would rather be anywhere else on earth? The answer lies in their initial response to the question posed by their mind/body system, which effectively asks: "Is the coming massive drop a threat to you?" For those who consider the roller-coaster a positive experience (due to nurture or inherited values, it doesn't matter), their response as the roller-coaster begins its first big descent is to smile, hold up a clenched fist and exhale with a cry of "ALL RIIIIIGHT!" This response communicates to their mind/body system that, far from their fight/flight response being required, they are treated instead to feel-good endorphins, making them feel exhilarated and on top of the world. Conversely, the person sitting next to them who responded to the same question by taking a deep breath and adopting a stricken expression is treated to the chemicals associated with their flight response. A panic attack is the worst-case scenario.

The power of exhalation!

An instant and powerful exhalation is the main way we communicate to our mind/body system that, far from feeling threatened, we are having a great time. Therefore, it rewards us with the chemicals necessary to experience this joyful/exhilarating experience to its fullest.

Five

The Folly

The folly of responding to ANYTHING by taking a breath

When we respond to something with an inhalation, it communicates that we are not having the best of times – for instance, the moment we receive bad news, when a car pulls out unexpectedly and we must brake suddenly, or when we trip and must prevent a fall. In fact, the moment we experience ANYTHING unpleasant, we react by drawing a breath, and this 'threat message' is relayed to our mind/body system. Therefore, we receive an injection of anxiety-or-dread-inducing chemicals into our mind/body system, one that corresponds to the severity of the inhalation and contraction of the diaphragm muscle.

Six

The Positive Response

You are now vaguely aware of what you need to do in response to surges of anxiety: utilise your Message Muscles to send *a new and positive message* that communicates, "Far from being threatened by these surges, I feel exhilarated by them!" Once mastered, you will move out of the roller-coaster's anxiety seat, and into one where you embrace the ride. In many ways, the roller-coaster is a metaphor for our daily lives.

I spent many years teaching people these responsive skills. During that time, the response evolved through several incarnations, before finally being built around the Balloon Method. The Balloon Method ticks all the boxes when it comes ensuring that the Message Muscles are doing *exactly* what they need to be doing to send a positive message that triggers the release of uplifting endorphins that flush the anxiety chemicals from your system.

Warning

While practising the following training exercises, you may feel light-headed, just as you would if you were blowing up real balloons. If so, use your common sense and take a break whenever necessary.

Let's start by blowing up three imaginary balloons
Place the tips of your thumb and forefinger on either side of your belly button and apply a little pressure so you can feel (**and be absolutely certain that**) your abdominal muscles are moving in as you blow up each imaginary balloon. The exhalation you're about to produce should be **strong and measured** (just as it would need to be if you were blowing up a real balloon), and it should last approximately five seconds. To avoid getting too light-headed, it is advised that you wait for at least thirty seconds in between blowing up your three imaginary balloons.

Time to blow up three imaginary balloons in the way described above.

During the above exercise, you should have felt how your abdominal muscles **moved inwards** as you blew air into your imaginary balloons. Of course, during your exhalation, your diaphragm would have automatically moved up into its most relaxed position. As your diaphragm does what it needs to do automatically during your exhalation, you need not concern yourself with that message muscle from now on. Your attention should be firmly on making sure that your abdominal muscles are **moving inwards and tightening** while blowing up your balloon. <u>This inward movement of the abs is central to your new message, and instructs your mind/body system to create feel-good endorphins just as it does when you laugh.</u>

Before moving on, you should have blown up several imaginary balloons as described above.

Seven

Feelings of anxiety:
From Threat to Laughing Stock

When you enter the upcoming Feel-Good Endorphin Zone, your abs, diaphragm and facial muscles will be in their happiest position as far as your mind/body system is concerned. Why the happiest? Think about the times when a friend has said something so funny that it's had you doubled over with laughter. At these times, your abdominal muscles will have tightened to the point where ALL THE AIR has been expelled from your lungs, and you literally can't breathe. At such times, with tears streaming down your face, you may start gesticulating to your friend to stop making you laugh because you need to steal a breath. The reason you need to steal a breath? ALL THE AIR has been expelled from your lungs by your mirth. With the possible exception of a coughing fit, your abdominal muscles ONLY CONTRACT IN THIS SEVERE WAY during these happiest of moments. This results in your body being treated to an injection of feel-good endorphins to match the happiness of the experience.

20

The Feel-Good Endorphin Zone is designed to allow you to **mimic perfectly** those occasions when you're laughing **so hysterically** that you can barely breathe. When you do this in response to feelings of anxiety, it communicates to your mind/body system that far from being threatened by these feelings (and the issues attached to them), that you now consider them the funniest, least threatening things to stumble sideways across the earth. For this new perspective, you'll be treated to an injection of feel-good endorphins that neutralise the anxiety.

Eight

Training Part 1:
Entering The Feel-Good Endorphin Zone

1. Make a prong out of your thumb and forefinger and place this prong either side of your belly button. As you did earlier, apply some pressure so you can **feel and be absolutely certain that** your abdominal muscles move in and tighten as you exhale.

2. You're about to blow up an imaginary balloon. Produce a **strong and sustained exhalation** (from your abs) just as you would need to if you were blowing up a real balloon: **keep blowing until you've expelled ALL the air from your lungs and your abs feel as tight as they would if you were laughing hysterically**. Now, holding your tightened abs in place **by not breathing air back into your stomach and applying a little pressure with your prong**, smile and **BREATHE SHALLOWLY FROM YOUR UPPER CHEST**.

3. If you have followed the above directions correctly, you will have **expelled AS MUCH air from your belly as you**

physically can, and you'll be **holding your tightened abs in place** by breathing into your UPPER CHEST and NOT YOUR STOMACH.

How long should you remain in the Feel-Good Endorphin Zone?
In the initial learning stages, you should remain in the Zone, your abs tightened to their **<u>fullest</u>** by your exhalation, and breathing into your upper chest, for approximately 10 seconds. Please practise entering the Feel-Good Endorphin Zone a few times before moving on.

Nine

Exiting the Feel-Good Endorphin Zone

While inside the Feel-Good Endorphin Zone, you will have been denying your body oxygen into your abdominal area, exactly as you do whenever you laugh hysterically. For this reason, when you leave the Zone by taking a normal breath (relaxing your abs) and breathing into your belly again, you'll discover that this initial breath is **naturally deep**, enjoyable, and brings a sense of relief. This is one of those few occasions when taking a deep breath feels and **is** great. Why? Because it provides the same sensation of relief as when, for instance, you have swum the length of a pool underwater, burst through the surface, and taken that first gulp of wonderful air. This need to take a big, refreshing gulp of air adds a sense of euphoria to the good work you've just done creating feel-good endorphins. This **need** to take a deep and relieving breath when you exit the Feel-Good Endorphin Zone is a good indication that you entered it successfully. In fact, the bigger the breath **you naturally need** to take when you leave the Zone indicates how far you journeyed into it. Clearly, the further the better as far as the production of feel-good endorphins is concerned and, equally as important, the strength of your new positive message that communicates, "I have NO need for any assistance from my fight/flight response!" If you exit the Zone and have no need to take a deep, relieving breath, it's an indication that you baulked, or else didn't apply the no-nonsense effort that is required when you enter the Zone. More on that shortly.

Ten

The Abdominal Screwdriver

How to ensure that your abs remain as tight as possible
while in the Feel-Good Endorphin Zone

While in the Zone, your mouth will be curled up into a grin,
and you'll be breathing shallowly from your upper chest.
To ensure that your abs remain as tight as possible, **use
them** (your abs) to puff and send quick bursts of air out of
your mouth that will FURTHER **tighten your abs**. Doing
this will provide you with, for want of a better term, a
valve that you can instantly use to squeeze the maximum
amount of feel-good endorphins from your abdominal
'sponge.'

The Feel-Good Endorphin Sponge

The **tightening and holding** of your tightened abs (as
though mid-hysterical laugh) is not only paramount to the
production of feel-good endorphins, but is also key to
sending the **all-important new message** regarding the

issues that have triggered your fight/flight response. It can therefore be useful to imagine that a sponge has been wrapped around your abdominal muscles and, the more you tighten them by exhaling **from** them, the greater the amount of feel-good endorphins you will squeeze from the sponge. Again, what you're doing here is mimicking what your abs, diaphragm (and face if you're smiling) are doing whenever you find something hysterically funny. With practice, you will discover that when squeezed to the maximum, this sponge has a **sweet spot** that takes the release of feel-good endorphins to another level. What is required from you to hit the sponge's sweet spot? Effort – **maximum effort** in blowing up your imaginary balloon and tightening your abs **just that little bit further** than you imagined possible

How long should you remain in the Feel Good Endorphin Zone?

Anywhere from five seconds to a couple of minutes. Practice makes perfect, and once you're adept at entering the Feel-Good Endorphin Zone, the world is your oyster as far as the creation of those endorphins is concerned.

Eleven

Time To Take Stock Of The anxiety

Once the euphoria of taking that big, relieving inhalation has passed when you exit the Zone, it's time to take stock of how you feel. It will depend **entirely** upon the amount of fight or flight response chemicals that were in your system when you entered the Feel-Good Endorphin Zone, as to how long it will take for them to be flushed out of it. A small amount will be dealt with instantly while in the Zone, but for severe levels of anxiety it **may take several minutes** for the feel-good endorphins you've just created to shepherd it away when you exit the Zone.

<u>Be alert to doubts during the shepherding process or they may be your undoing!</u>

Because large levels of flight chemicals can take several minutes to be expelled from your mind/body system, it gives the voice in the back of your mind the **perfect opportunity** to send doubts up to your conscious screen.

Doubts such as: "You just did exactly what he said and you still feel anxious! Told you it was too good to be true!" **Be aware that these doubts and any others like them are coming from this voice**. It sends them because it would much rather you erred on the side of caution and took flight from the issues that have triggered your anxiety as usual. Stand your ground against these doubts, and reply to them by reminding yourself that the shepherding process is underway. Do not entertain these doubts as doing so will partially erode the good work you've just done in the Zone.

Twelve

The Focus of Our Attention

In attempting not to entertain doubts in the minute or two after you exit the Zone, it is useful to be aware that our attention switches back and forth between two places:

1. Thinking and mulling things over (this obviously includes contemplating negative thoughts and doubts).

2. Paying attention to things externally in our surroundings.

It's impossible, for instance, to follow what's happening in a movie *and* be thinking about something at the same instant. If you've got something troubling on your mind then, throughout the movie, your attention will be switching back and forth between the movie (externally) and the issue internally on your mind. It's as though a magnetic arrow switches our attention back and forth between the two. This is why we are drawn to great entertainment; it provides us with the opportunity to relax and regroup by focusing our attention on something external for a while. So, the key here when attempting to ignore doubts when you leave the Feel-Good Endorphin Zone (and the shepherding of the flight chemicals out of your system is underway) is to try and keep the magnetic arrow of your attention external for a minute or two. This is best achieved by concentrating on the sights/sounds in your environment. It's not easy. The voice in the back of your mind will fight you tooth and nail to get you to consider its doubts concerning your new course of action (I. e., rejecting its offer of fight or flight response chemicals). But the more you can stand your ground and keep the focus of your attention on something external by say, studying the details of a picture on your wall, listening to some relaxing/empowering music, or focusing on an object in the distance if you're walking down the street, the more proficient you will become at this skill. In many ways, it's like developing a mind muscle that you can use to improve your external concentration. The best exponents of this skill are top 100 metre runners whose focus is on the finishing line throughout the race. Athletes refer to this level of unmolested (by thought) concentration as being in the zone.

Back to business: several minutes **have** passed now since I left the Zone, and I still don't feel 100%

This means that more feel-good endorphin troops are required on the battlefield. Remember, you have an **unlimited supply** at your disposal, so re-enter the Zone, squeeze that sponge for **all you're worth, and once again command your mind/body system to provide you with the endorphins you need**. Remember, your mind/body system has been programmed by nature to release endorphins whenever your abdominal and diaphragm muscles contract in this positive and decisive way. This extreme level of effort is only required in the initial stages of sorting out your **over-protective** flight response regarding an issue. Slowly but surely, your mind/body system will get the message that you're fully out of danger regarding the issue, and once it does, your battle against these feelings of anxiety (in relation to it) will be consigned to the past. Like anything else in life, the more effort you put in, the quicker the job is done.

Thirteen

Zero Tolerance Towards anxiety!

New York City was once the most crime-ridden and dangerous city in the United States –until a forward-thinking mayor brought in a Zero Tolerance policy towards crime. From that moment on, even the smallest of misdemeanours – dropping litter and jaywalking – were punished mercilessly. It turned New York into one of safest cities in the U.S. Zero tolerance is **precisely** the policy you need to adopt towards **any** feeling of anxiety. Reply to them with your balloon response and squeeze every of drop of feel-good endorphins from the sponge. Once again: **your mind/body system has AN UNLIMITED supply of feel-good endorphins to put at your disposal**. Their positive effects never diminish. So why allow any feelings of anxiety to go unchecked? Squeeze your abdominal sponge and force your mind/body system to produce endorphins to replace the flight chemicals. Another way to look at is this: when set upon by anxiety, you can either fight back with the weapons you now have at your disposal, or passively submit to them. It's true that a component of the flight response is designed to render you passive. To make you feel hopeless. **This feeling is an illusion**. You <u>can</u> fight back. You must fight back. Send your mind/body system a new message. The quality of your life depends upon your doing so.

<u>What you're thinking when you enter the Feel-Good Endorphin Zone</u>

Words are powerful things with powerful overtones. While a compliment can lift our spirits, an insult can bring us down with a bump. With this in mind, it certainly can't hurt to send a **positive mental response** as well as the physical one when blowing up the balloon and entering the Zone. For instance, repeating a mantra such as, 'I'm fine! I'm fine! I'm fine!" They say that the best form of defence is attack, and this is certainly true when it comes to dealing with anxiety. So, taking the fight <u>to</u> the anxiety by beckoning it on and thinking, "Come on! Come on! COME ON!" while blowing up the balloon and entering the Zone can be highly effective.

The precise words are something you can experiment with.

Choose a mantra that has the most positive resonance with you.

Mimicking mirth

Similarly, when blowing up the balloon and entering the Feel-Good Endorphin Zone (when alone), it can be beneficial to do so with an exhalation where you say '*Heeeeeeeee!*' under your breath.

A quick demonstration

Place the prong of your thumb and forefinger either side of your belly button. Now impersonate Muttley's (from *Wacky Races*) laugh by hissing '*he, he, he, he, he,*' and feel how markedly your abdominal muscles move in towards the sweet spot of the sponge. It's no coincidence that this sound is close to an actual laugh. With this in mind, you may discover that blowing up your balloon with a hissed, five-second '*Heeeeeeeee!*' is more effective for tightening your abs to their maximum than by simply blowing up the balloon in the usual way.

Again, when alone, some people also find that producing a low growl while blowing up the balloon can be empowering. Others like to squeeze a sports hand grip to the closed position as they exhale and blow up their imaginary balloon. Experiment and go with what feels the most effective for you: the most important thing is that you grow adept at <u>contracting your abdominal muscles by exhaling FROM THEM</u>, holding them tightly in place, and then using the air that you're breathing into your chest to exhale and tighten them some more. Think ratchet. The greater the ratcheting of your abdominal muscles (which mimics what they do when you're laughing hysterically or being thrilled by a roller-coaster ride) the greater the production of feel-good endorphins for the battlefield. Once inside the Feel-Good Endorphin Zone, the air you are breathing into your **upper chest** provides the perfect ammunition for this ratcheting process.

<u>Greater physical strength</u>

You will also discover that when you exhale from your abs (and hold them) prior to lifting something, that you will be provided with significantly more strength. This extra strength is testament to the good place your mind/body system enters **whenever** you utilise your abdominal muscles in this positive way. Clearly, exhaling in this manner during exercise is going to produce massive amounts of feel-good endorphins. Well done the medical community for advising people who suffer from depression to engage in physical exercise!

Fourteen

Training Part 2:
The Lesser Golf-Ball-Sized Balloon Response.

While determination to blow up a full-size imaginary balloon (and enter the Feel-Good Endorphin Zone) is required when addressing full-on waves of anxiety, a less heavy-duty response is required when encountering moments when you experience much smaller twangs of anxiety. These twangs are akin to a single butterfly of anxiety entering your belly. In the past, you would have reacted to this butterfly by **taking** a breath. This breath had the effect of drawing more butterflies in to join the first. Depending on the level of distraction you had at that moment, this single butterfly might have escalated to full blown Free-Fall. Clearly, the best course of action is to **instantly expel** the butterfly, and then enter a far less intense version of the Feel-Good Endorphin Zone. This is most effectively achieved by replacing the full-sized imaginary balloon with a golf-ball-sized balloon.

A balloon the size of a golf ball would require only

require a **single, sharp puff of air** to inflate – a short, sharp burst that instantly expels the butterfly. So, let's try that now. Place your prong either side of your belly button (to ensure the inward movement of your abs when you exhale) and blow up a golf-ball-sized balloon with a **single and decisive** exhalation that lasts half a second. Now hold your **slightly tightened abs** in place and breathe in and out through your nose into your chest, thereby ensuring that the butterfly (of anxiety) you have just expelled cannot return there. The presence of that single butterfly in your belly was an indication that the voice in the back of your mind has just prodded you gently and enquired, "I don't suppose there's any chance that you're feeling threatened by *these* issues now?" The golf-ball-sized response will tell it: "No, there isn't!" This mini version of the Feel-Good Endorphin Zone is a great place to be in general. I automatically go there whenever I'm experiencing a stressful time. Since it's entered using a quick exhalation that produces only a **<u>minor tightening</u>** of the abs, it's not in the least bit uncomfortable, and yet produces low levels of feel-good endorphins that help to keep you calm and focused. Like I said, it's a great space to inhabit. **And**

worth experimenting with when taking stock having just exited the full-on Feel-Good Endorphin Zone. And remember! While in this mini version of the Zone, it's important that you hold your **slightly tightened abs** in place, breathe in and out of **your chest**, and have a slight smile on your lips that suits the more considered nature of this mini zone. What's more, due to its more relaxed nature, you can remain in it for as long as you like. Doing so will enable you to provide your mind/body system with low levels of feel-good endorphins all day long if you wish. As well as keeping harmful anxiety chemicals at bay (by keeping the fight/flight response in check), you'll be creating feel-good endorphins that boost your immune system and assist in keeping you healthy.

Fifteen

Beware of Baulking!

This brings us to the only thing that now stands between you and a life free of your flight response constantly erring on the side of caution and causing the release of those chemicals that are responsible for your anxiety: baulking. What is baulking? If a racehorse approaches a difficult fence that it doesn't think it can get over, it will come to an abrupt halt, sometimes throwing its rider to the ground. This means the horse has *baulked* at the idea of jumping the fence. If you abandon your plan to enter the Feel-Good Endorphin Zone and allow the anxiety chemicals free rein as before, it will be because of the myriad of doubts that flew into your mind and told you to give up and throw in the towel – that resisting this tidal wave of anxiety is futile. The old and predictable favourites that the voice in the back of your mind will use will include: "Are you *crazy*? What are you *doing*? This is NEVER going to work! It's much too difficult! You haven't got the strength!" etc.

By far the best way of dealing with negativity is to turn it into positivity, by using its own weight against it. This is achieved by looking upon surges of anxiety not as things to recoil from as in the past, but as **prompts and reminders** to enter either the full-on Feel-Good Endorphin Zone and **squeeze that sponge**, or else to utilise the mini zone, and produce lower levels of feel-good endorphins over a longer period. If you adjust your mindset to respond to feelings of anxiety in this way, and make them **your triggers to do something positive**, you'll tear this previously inhibiting barrier down. The good news is that getting into the habit of responding to anxiety in this new way, is far easier to achieve than you imagine. You just have to decide that that's what you're going to do, stick to your guns, and engage your mind/body system in this new and positive way.

Sixteen

An Important Realisation

The voice in the back of your mind can only *persuade* you to surrender your new response by convincing you to baulk. **IT CAN'T MAKE YOU**. The power is ultimately with you to enter the Feel-Good Endorphin Zone when you feel threatened by **unwelcome and entirely counter-productive** feelings of anxiety.

Seventeen

Practise

Practise makes perfect, and practising going into the Zone will stand you in good stead for when you need it. Ideally, once you've mastered your two new responses (full-sized balloon response and golf-ball-sized balloon response) you will have someone who can assist you in practising them. This is best achieved by asking your helper to stand behind you. After a period of time has passed (anything from a few seconds to a minute) they should grab your shoulder and attempt to startle you. This grab/startle represents the moment that *that* question is posed and you feel suddenly under threat from a wave of anxiety. When they grab your shoulder, it's your cue to instantly exhale from your abs and blow up your balloon, to smile, and to shallow-breathe into your chest.

Eighteen

Learning From Any Initial Confusion

The first few times you attempt to go into the Feel-Good Endorphin Zone when under attack from anxiety, the voice in the back of your mind may well be successful in convincing you to baulk, or to put in a half-hearted effort. If this happens, **do not get disheartened**. This is your opportunity to learn. Think about what you did during those vital few seconds when you were *supposed* to enter the Zone. Think about the doubts it used to deter you, and **be alert** and ready for them the next time. You will soon learn to stick to your guns, enter the Zone, and squeeze the life out of the sponge **regardless**. The alternative? Passively allowing the flight response free rein to overreact and produce those anxiety chemicals that bring you to your knees? NO LONGER ACCEPTABLE. The time has come to send your mind/body system a new message: "The threats are miles away now! I'm feeling invigorated! So give me the good stuff!"

Part 2

Getting to Know the Voice

Throughout this book, I have referred to the voice in the back of your mind – the one that effectively asks: "Are the things associated with <u>this</u> feeling of anxiety a threat to you?" An understanding of what this voice is and why it asks the question will be useful in helping you to stick to your guns when dealing with it.

So, what is the Voice? The Voice is an individual memory cell, one of countless others in your mind. I like to call these memory cells OASES, as they resemble tiny pools of electrical energy that store your memories. The overwhelming majority of your oases are friendly and useful. For instance, if you own a dog, it will be the job of your Dog Oasis to store and safeguard any information about your dog. What's more, this oasis is tasked with delivering this information about your dog to your conscious 'screen' when you want it or when it's appropriate. For instance, your Dog Oasis is responsible for reminding you when it's time to feed or walk your dog. If you forget to do either, it will be because ANOTHER, STRONGER OASIS in your mind has sent what it considers to be more pressing information to your screen, and got you thinking about the information inside its 'file.' As a result, your Dog Oasis is shut out from your screen and must wait its turn before bursting back and reminding you that, "You were supposed to walk the dog an hour ago!"

These individual oases battle for our attention throughout the day (and night in the form of dreams), which explains why we always have SOMETHING on our mind. They like nothing better than for us to mull over the information inside their file. Why? Because the more time we spend dwelling on the information about a specific person, place or thing inside the file of an oasis, the more electrical energy we supply it, and the bigger and stronger it will grow. What's more, for a dominant oasis to remain so, it needs to bully its way back onto your screen and coax you into thinking about the information (person, place or thing) inside its file AS OFTEN AS IT CAN. It achieves this by asking you questions that tempt you into its file. It is being unaware of the ploys your individual oases use to tempt us back into their files that results in our wasting time obsessing over things we'd be **much better off** ignoring. The following Lost in the Desert Analogy will help you to understand more clearly how your oases also attempt to influence your decision-making process throughout the day.

Twenty

The Desert Analogy

A man is lost in the desert. The poor man is desperately tired, but also desperately thirsty, so he will have two opposing oases in his mind: his Rest Oasis and his Thirst Oasis. His Rest Oasis, which is responsible for making sure he doesn't die of exhaustion, will be telling him, "Stop now and rest! You're exhausted!"

Meanwhile, the man's Thirst Oasis, which is tasked with making sure he doesn't die of thirst, will be muscling in on his screen and telling him, "No. Don't stop. Keep walking and find water, otherwise you're going to die of thirst!" These opposing oases will battle for supremacy in his mind, and attempt to persuade him to follow *their* instructions to either rest or to struggle on and find water.

That was a simple example to help you understand how your oases attempt to influence your decision-making process throughout the day. The longer you allow two opposing oases free rein to put their arguments to you on your conscious screen, the longer it will take you to make a decision, and the more drained you will feel.

Twenty one

The Ringmaster

<u>An important realisation that will lessen your stress levels and greatly improve your quality of life</u>

Although your oases are a part of you, they are also separate from you (the screen). In this respect you are a bit like a ringmaster, and your oases are the lions you need to keep under control. Paying attention to and observing how your individual oases attempt to get you thinking (and stressing over) the information inside their files will increase your understanding of how your mind works, making you a better ringmaster. The better a ringmaster you are, the less your oases will have free rein to coax you their files to re-tread the same old ground in search of the 'answers' to your anxiety. Fact: the answers are NEVER located in these files. They contain only **the same** questions to mull over **yet again, and what's more the act of considering these questions will often trigger your fight/flight response**. So, to reiterate: while your oases are a part of you, they are also separate from you (the screen).

This truth is never more obvious than when a subject you'd **much rather not think about** keeps returning to your screen and refuses to leave you alone. Another useful analogy would be those times when you can hear a recording of a song playing on your screen. It may be a song you absolutely hate, but no matter how much you try to get rid of it, it outstays its welcome and continues to play. YOU WOULD NEVER THINK ABOUT A SONG YOU CAN'T STAND BY CHOICE. This alone is incontrovertible proof that these oases are separate from you, and in case you were wondering why that infernal song refuses to leave, it's because it enjoys the feed of electrical activity it receives while on your screen, just like all your other oases do. The voice in the back of your mind is your Trip-Wire Oasis. Why? Because it keeps attempting to trip you up with its basic question, "Are the things associated with *these* feeling of anxiety a threat to you?" You now know how to send the emphatic reply: "NO THEY ARE NOT!"

In Conclusion

<u>A vital resource</u>

This book is short for a reason. I have endeavoured to stick to the salient points to make them easy to find. My advice would be to read through it several times, and jot down the things that resonate with you the most.

I would like to wish you all the best with putting an end to your anxiety. If you have any questions that you feel have not been answered in this book, you are welcome to email me at <u>boyd.brent1@gmail.com</u>

It will be a pleasure to assist you in any way I can.

Fight
<u>NOT</u>
Flight!

The Key To Preventing Panic Attacks

Boyd Brent

Contact: <u>boyd.brent1@gmail.com</u>

Introduction

Your body is a feel-good endorphin making powerhouse. It's able to provide you with an unlimited supply of feel-good endorphins throughout your life. At the same time, it can also manufacture those fight or flight response chemicals that are 100% responsible for causing your panic attacks. Both of these, fight or flight chemicals and feel-good endorphins, are produced by the same glands in our bodies, the same extraordinary powerhouse. This book will provide you with the skills you need to switch off your fight/flight response whenever a panic attack threatens, and **prompt** your body into producing feel-good endorphins instead. A decade's worth of research has been sieved down to include only those no-nonsense, practical skills you need to achieve this. I developed the skills you're about to learn as a means of understanding and putting an end to my own panic attacks, and then spent a decade teaching them to clients who visited my clinic in London.

1. Understanding Panic Attack Free-Fall!

You're feeling okay when you experience a sinking feeling and a voice in the back of your mind basically asks: "Is the idea of having a panic attack RIGHT NOW a threat to you?"

To compensate for this sudden sinking feeling, you begin taking deeper breaths, and your face adopts an anxious expression.

The voice in the back of your mind probes you again: "Is there ANY CHANCE that having a panic attack right now is NOT a threat?"

Your growing mental and physical distress tells it: "No! There's no chance whatsoever!"

Your FLIGHT RESPONSE is now fully activated, flooding your body with the chemicals that are 100% responsible for causing your panic attacks.

This process of Panic Attack Free-Fall is a vicious circle: more often than not, it's the fear of having a panic attack that is *causing* further panic attacks. Without an entirely different response to the question that triggers them – one that sends a message of reassurance: "I'm fine! I have no need of my flight response at this time!" – this vicious circle of panic attacks will continue.

2. The Physical Message

Only a powerful PHYSICAL MESSAGE of positivity/reassurance will convince your mind/body system to do a 180° turn, and manufacture feel-good endorphins instead of fight or flight chemicals. Millions of years of evolution has taught it to trust your physical response to things you encounter (this includes your thoughts and memories as well as things in the outside world) as to whether it will either:

A. Pump fight or flight chemicals into your system that make you want to escape the situation (panic attacks).

B. Treat you to exhilarating, feel-good endorphins that make you want to seek out the experience again.

The good news is that your mind/body system has evolved to trust your physical response **completely**. Why is this good news? Because it has no idea that you are about to learn the skills necessary to send it the positive physical message that it understands and listens for. This message will tell it, "The panic attack threat is no longer an issue! I have no need of my flight response at this time!" This new response will quash any feelings of burgeoning anxiety, and prevent them from escalating into a panic attack.

It's time to introduce you to the all-important muscles that send this positive message of reassurance: the aptly-named Message Muscles …

3. The Message Muscles

The Message Muscles are the muscles that your mind/body system monitors. They are the muscles that it assesses to ascertain whether to pump fight/flight chemicals or feel-good endorphins into your system. Our Message Muscles are located in three areas in our bodies:

Message Muscle no. 1: the Face

The most obvious, but by **no means the most important,** are the muscles in your face, which conspire to contort your features into an expression of fear. This can only communicate one thing to your mind/body system: "Yes! I feel threatened and need my flight response!" But the facial muscles are small-fry when compared to the second message muscle, and it's no accident that it's one of the biggest and most flexible muscles in the human body: the diaphragm.

Message Muscle no. 2: the Diaphragm

Your diaphragm is located inside your rib cage, resembling a giant elastic band that stretches horizontally from one side of your rib cage to the other. Whenever you breathe in, your diaphragm moves down and, as it does so, it assists in sucking air into your lungs. The longer you inhale, the further down your diaphragm travels towards your waist, and the tenser and more uncomfortable it and you feel.

Take a long, slow, deep breath.

Unpleasant, wasn't it? This is because when we breathe in, our diaphragm is pulled down and stretched into its most taut position. When we breathe out again, we experience a feeling of relief. Much of this relief is due to the diaphragm moving back up into a relaxed position.

Message Muscle no. 3: the Abdominal Muscles

The third and final set of message muscles are the abdominal muscles. The abdominal muscles are as important as the diaphragm in sending a message that will avert a panic attack. In these fitness-obsessed times, we are all aware of where our abs are located, but let's reacquaint ourselves with them now. Bring a thumb and forefinger on the same hand together so that they touch, then draw them apart slowly to create a prong. Take this prong (your thumb and forefinger) and place it against your abs (horizontally) either side of your belly button. Now exhale forcibly and feel how your abs move inwards as you do.

An important realisation

Whenever we are involved in an enjoyable, uplifting activity, the emphasis of our breathing is ALWAYS on the exhalation – when we laugh, cheer, sing, whistle a tune, or groan because we're enjoying a good massage. During all these activities (and ANY OTHER pleasurable activity you can think of), the emphasis of our breathing is *always* on the exhalation, never on the inhalation. Let's take this analogy to its ultimate conclusion: the Roller-coaster Ride …

4. The Roller-coaster Ride

Some people love roller-coasters, getting a high when riding them, while for others, they can represent their worst nightmare. What dictates why some people love the feeling of that first uncontrollable plunge, while others would rather be anywhere else on earth? The answer lies in their initial response to the question posed by their Roller-coaster Oasis, which basically asks: "Is the coming massive drop a threat to you?" For those who consider the roller-coaster a positive experience (due to nurture or inherited values, it really doesn't matter), their response as the roller-coaster begins its first big descent is to smile, hold up a clenched fist, and exhale with a cry of "ALL RIIIIIIGHT!" This response communicates that far from their flight response being required at this time, they are instead treated to a wholly different set of chemicals, which make them feel exhilarated and on top of the world. Conversely, the person sitting next to them who responded to the same question by taking a deep breath and adopting a stricken expression is treated to the chemicals associated with their FLIGHT response. A panic attack is the worst-case scenario.

The power of exhalation!

An instant and powerful exhalation is the main way we communicate to our mind/body system that, far from feeling threatened, we are having a great time. This is why it rewards us with the chemicals necessary to experience this joyful/exhilarating experience to its fullest.

5. The Folly

<u>The folly of responding to ANYTHING by taking a deep breath</u>

When we respond to something with an inhalation, it communicates that we are not having the best of times. For instance, the moment we receive bad news, when a car pulls out unexpectedly and we have to brake suddenly, or when we trip and have to catch our fall. In fact, the moment we experience ANYTHING unpleasant, we react by drawing a breath, and this 'threat message' is relayed to our Fight/Flight response. This is why we receive an injection of anxiety-inducing chemicals into our mind/body system, one that corresponds to the severity of the inhalation and contraction of the diaphragm muscle.

6. Positive Response Training

You are now vaguely aware of what you need to do prevent a panic attack when you feel under threat of having one: utilise your Message Muscles to send an overwhelmingly positive message that communicates, "I feel great and have no need of my flight response at this time, thanks!"

I spent six years teaching people these responsive skills in my practice in London. During that time, the response evolved through several incarnations, before finally being built around the Balloon Method. The Balloon Method ticks all the boxes when it comes ensuring that the Message Muscles are doing *exactly* what they need to be doing in order to stamp out a potential panic attack.

Warning

While practising the following training exercises, you may feel light-headed, just as you would if you were blowing up real balloons. If so, use your common sense and take a break whenever necessary.

Let's start by blowing up three imaginary balloons

Place the tips of your thumb and forefinger on either side of your belly button and apply a little pressure so you can feel **(and be absolutely certain that)** your abdominal muscles moving in as you blow up each imaginary balloon. The exhalation you're about to produce should be strong and measured (just as it would need to be if you were blowing up a real balloon), and it should last approximately five seconds. To avoid getting too light-headed, it is advised that you wait for at least thirty seconds in between blowing up your three imaginary balloons.

Time to blow up three imaginary balloons in the way described above.

During the above exercise, you should have felt how your abdominal muscles **moved inwards** as you blew air into your imaginary balloons. Of course, during your exhalation, your diaphragm would have automatically moved up into its most relaxed position. As your diaphragm does what it needs to do automatically during your exhalation, you need not concern yourself with that message muscle from now on. Your attention should be firmly on making sure that your abdominal muscles are **moving inwards and tightening** while blowing up your balloon. <u>This inward movement of the abs is central to your new message, and instructs your mind/body system to create feel-good endorphins just as it does when you laugh</u>.

Before moving on to the next section, you should have blown up several imaginary balloons as described above. Once mastered, you'll be ready to move into the Panic Attack Safe Zone ...

7. The Panic Attack Safe Zone

The Panic Attack Safe Zone is a place where having a panic attack is physically impossible. Why impossible? In order for your body to trigger and run a panic attack, **it needs you** to supply it with the extra oxygen that makes a panic attack possible. If you refuse to supply it with this extra oxygen, it CANNOT go into panic attack mode. If this sounds like a comforting realization, it ought to be. It means that ultimately the power is in your hands to either allow **or prevent** panic attacks from occurring.

The energy/oxygen that's needed and expended during a panic attack

In the wake of past panic attacks, you will have been left feeling shaky, weak and tired. This is due to the extraordinary amount of energy/oxygen that our bodies must burn to trigger and sustain a panic attack.

Your body's reliance on available oxygen resources

When you are feeling fine and breathing normally, the air you are breathing is being used to run your bodily functions. Your mind/body system requires this oxygen to sustain your organs and keep things ticking over nicely. It cannot afford to divert oxygen away from your heart or brain or any vital organ in order to engage in the luxury of a panic attack. This is why it **REQUIRES you to breathe deeply** and supply it with this extra oxygen. Just as a car's engine cannot run without petrol, so a panic attack cannot run without you breathing extra oxygen into your lungs. For this reason, the Panic Attack Safe Zone that you're soon to practise entering is a place where:

1. You have just forcibly expelled **all the air** from your lungs with your balloon response.

2. You are holding your **tightened abdominal muscles** in place.

3. You have slowed your breathing down to a bare minimum.

8. Panic Attacks: From Threat to Laughing Stock

<u>Before we get to the Panic Attack Safe Zone training, it is explained further</u>

Once inside the Panic Attack Safe Zone, your abs, diaphragm and facial muscles will be in their happiest position as far as your mind/body system is concerned. Why the happiest? Think about those times when a friend has said something so funny that it's had you doubled over with laughter. At these times, your abdominal muscles will have tightened to the point where ALL THE AIR has been expelled from your lungs, and you literally can't breathe. At such times, with tears streaming down your face, you may start gesticulating to your friend to stop making you laugh because you need to steal a breath. The reason you need to steal a breath? ALL THE AIR has been expelled from your lungs by your mirth. With the possible exception of a coughing fit, your abdominal muscles ONLY CONTRACT IN THIS SEVERE WAY during these happiest of moments. This results in your body being treated to an injection of feel-good endorphins to match the happiness of the experience. Let's try this now in a tiny way. Do your best Santa impersonation by saying loudly, "HO! HO! HO! HO!" and feel how your abs move in and tighten with each progressive "HO!"

In many ways, the purpose of the Panic Attack Safe Zone is to mimic those times when we are laughing so hysterically that we can barely breathe. When this is done at the start of Free-Fall (when you feel under threat from a panic attack), not only will you be denying your body the extra oxygen it needs to trigger and sustain a panic attack, but you will also communicate to your mind/body system that far from being threatened by the panic attack, you now consider it the funniest, least threatening thing that ever stumbled sideways across the earth. For this new perspective you'll be treated to an injection of uplifting, feel-good endorphins – and trust me, when you snuff out your first panic attack in this way, you will feel good!

9. Entering the Panic Attack Safe Zone

Once again, the Safe Zone is that place you inhabit where it is physically impossible to experience a panic attack.

<u>Entering The Safe Zone Training</u>

1. Make a prong out of your thumb and forefinger and place this prong either side of your belly button. As you did earlier, apply some pressure so you can **feel and be absolutely certain that** your abdominal muscles move in and tighten as you exhale.

2. You're about to blow up an imaginary balloon. Produce a **strong and sustained exhalation** (from your abs) just as you would need to if you were blowing up a real balloon: **keep blowing until you've expelled ALL the air from your lungs and your abs feel as tight as they would if you were laughing hysterically**. Now, holding your tightened abs in place **by not breathing air back into your stomach and applying a little pressure with your prong**, smile and **BREATHE SHALLOWLY FROM YOUR UPPER CHEST**.

3. If you have followed the above directions correctly, you will have **expelled AS MUCH air from your belly as you physically can,** and you'll be **holding your tightened abs in place** by breathing into your UPPER CHEST and NOT YOUR STOMACH.

This is Safe Zone. In this Zone, your mind/body system is being forced to devote the oxygen **you are allowing it** to maintaining your normal bodily functions. This is why it's impossible for your body to produce a panic attack. What is more, having responded to the threat of having a panic attack in this positive way, your mind/body system will get the message that your flight response is **not** required at this time. Far from it! Because your diaphragm, face and abdominal muscles are mimicking what they do when you find something hysterically funny, you will be telling it that you now find the threat of having a panic attack a joke.

How long should you remain in your Safe Zone?
Typically, 5-15 seconds spent in your Safe Zone is all that's required to send this new message and avert a panic attack. Should you leave your Safe Zone and feel threatened by a panic attack again, this is your mind/body

system asking you, "Are you *sure* the lion is laughable now?" If this occurs, you obviously respond to this enquiry by returning to your Safe Zone and remaining there for a few more seconds. During my time teaching people this response in person, it was unheard of for anyone to have to return to their Safe Zone for a third time.

10. Exiting the Panic Attack Safe Zone

While inside the Panic Attack Safe Zone, you will have been denying your body oxygen into your abdominal area, exactly as you do whenever you laugh hysterically. For this reason, when you leave the Zone by taking a normal breath (relaxing your abs) and breathing into your belly again, you'll discover that this initial breath is **naturally deep**, enjoyable, and brings a sense of relief. This is one of those few occasions when taking a deep breath feels and **is** great. Why? Because it provides the same sensation of relief as when, for instance, you have swum the length of a pool underwater, burst through the surface, and taken that first gulp of wonderful air. This need to take a big, refreshing gulp of air adds a sense of euphoria to the good work you've just done creating feel-good endorphins. This **need** to take a deep and relieving breath when you exit the Panic Attack Safe Zone is a good indication that you entered it successfully. In fact, the bigger the breath **you naturally need** to take when you leave the Zone indicates how far you journeyed into it. Clearly, the further the better as far as the production of feel-good endorphins is concerned and, equally as important, the strength of your new positive message that communicates, "I have NO need for any assistance from my fight/flight response!" If you exit the Zone and have no need to take a deep, relieving breath, it's an indication that you baulked, or else didn't apply the no-nonsense effort that is required when you enter the Zone. More on that shortly.

11. The Abdominal Screwdriver

<u>How to ensure that your abs remain as tight as possible while in the Panic Attack Safe Zone</u>

While in the Zone, your mouth will be curled up into a grin, and you'll be breathing shallowly from your upper chest. To ensure that your abs remain as tight as possible, **use them** (your abs) to puff and send quick bursts of air out of your mouth that will FURTHER **tighten your abs**. Doing this will provide you with, for want of a better term, a valve that you can instantly use to squeeze the maximum amount of feel-good endorphins from your abdominal 'sponge.'

<u>The Feel-Good Endorphin Sponge</u>
The **tightening and holding** of your tightened abs (as though mid-hysterical laugh) is not only paramount to the production of feel-good endorphins, but is also key to snuffing out a panic attack. It can therefore be useful to imagine that a sponge has been wrapped around your

abdominal muscles and, the more you tighten them by exhaling **from** them, the greater the amount of feel-good endorphins you will squeeze from the sponge. Again, what you're doing here is mimicking what your abs, diaphragm (and face if you're smiling) are doing whenever you find something hysterically funny. With practice, you will discover that when squeezed to the maximum, this sponge has a **sweet spot** that takes the release of panic attack dousing feel-good endorphins to another level. What is required from you to hit the sponge's sweet spot? Effort – **maximum effort** in blowing up your imaginary balloon and tightening your abs **just that little bit further** than you imagined possible.

12. Beware of Baulking!

You now know what you need to do to put an end to your panic attacks. The *moment* that question at the start of Free-Fall is posed and you experience those initial jitters/butterflies, you need to shut down your fight/flight response by entering your Safe Zone – a place where having a panic attack is physically impossible.

This brings us to the only thing that thing that now stands between you and a life free of panic attacks: baulking. What is baulking? If a racehorse approaches a difficult fence, one it doesn't think it can get over, it will come to an abrupt halt, sometimes throwing its rider to the ground. This means the horse has *baulked* at the idea of jumping the fence. If you abandon your plan to enter the Safe Zone and revert to breathing deeply as before, it will be because of the myriad of doubts that flew into your mind and told you to give up and throw in the towel – that resisting this tidal wave of anxiety is futile. The old and predictable favourites that the voice in the back of your mind will use to make you do this will be: "Are you *crazy*? What are you *doing*? This is NEVER going to work! It's much too difficult! You haven't got the strength!" etc.

THESE DOUBTS AND ANY OTHERS ARE NOT YOUR OWN. The voice in the back of you mind has sent them in order to destroy your resolve and make you revert to your old response. Why? After months or even years of telling it that panic attacks are a serious threat, when you begin to tell it something different it will want to be sure. This is why it **may** initially ask you the question again shortly after you leave your Safe Zone. If so, simply return to your Safe Zone for another few seconds to let the Trip-Wire Oasis know that you are indeed sure.

13. One Final And Important Realisation

The voice in the back of you mind can only *persuade* you to surrender your new response by convincing you to baulk. **IT CAN'T MAKE YOU**. The power is ultimately with you to enter your Safe Zone when you feel threatened by a panic attack: stopping it.

14. Practice

Practice makes perfect, and practicing going into your Safe Zone will stand you in good stead for when you need it. Ideally, once you've mastered your new response, you will have someone who can assist you in practicing it. This is best achieved by asking your helper to stand behind you. After a period of time has passed (anything from a few seconds to a minute) they should grab your shoulder and attempt to startle you. This grab/startle represents the moment that *that* question is posed and you feel suddenly under threat from a panic attack. **When they grab your shoulder, it's your cue to instantly exhale from your abs and blow up your balloon, to smile, and to shallow-breathe through your nose into your chest for 5-15 seconds**.

In Conclusion

I would like to wish you all the best with putting an end to your panic attacks. If you have any questions that you feel have not been answered in this book, you are welcome to email me at boyd.brent1@gmail.com

It will be a pleasure to assist you in any way I can.

Made in the USA
Middletown, DE
08 August 2022